A SIMPLE GUIDE TO CHESS

by

Sharon K. Rasmussen

Media Productions & Marketing
Lincoln, Nebraska

ISBN 0-9643353-0-1

This book is dedicated to my son Brian who inspired me to write this book and to my parents, Dr. William T. and Dorothy L. Kemp for their love and encouragement.

TABLE OF CONTENTS

Part 1
Rules and Strategy

CHAPTER 1

RULES OF CHESS

Chess is for two players, one person having the white pieces, and one person having the black pieces. The chessboard has sixty-four alternating light and dark squares.

Files. The vertical rows are called files.

Ranks. The horizontal rows are called ranks.

Before you begin your game, both players should make sure they have a white square at the right-hand corner of the board. The queens always start on a square of their color and are opposite each other.

At the beginning of the game, the pieces are in the positions shown in the diagram:

white square— 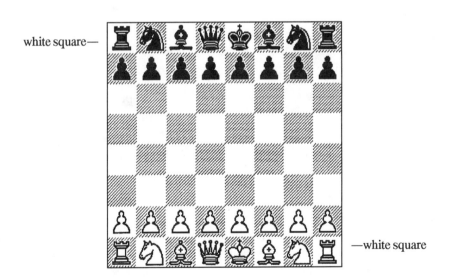 —white square

The Objective of Chess

The purpose of the game is to attack your opponent's king, making it impossible for your opponent to stop your attack. A move that attacks a king is called check. The king must escape on his next move if he can. If the king is in check and cannot move out of check; and if it is not possible to capture the attacking piece or to move one of his own pieces between the king and the attacking piece, then he is in checkmate and the game is over.

Drawn Games

Not all chess games are won or lost. Certain situations result in a draw:

- Stalemate—when the king is not in check, but the only possible move on the board would put him in check.

- Perpetual check—when a player can subject the opponent's king to an endless series of checks.

- By mutual agreement—after thirty moves have been made by both players.

- Fifty-move rule—when fifty moves have been made by both players without checkmate having been given, and without any piece having been captured or pawn moved.

- Repetition—when the same position (of all pieces, white and black) is repeated three times, with the same player having the move each time. On the third occurrence, this player may claim a draw; however, he must claim a draw before the position is changed by further play.

Move and Capture Rules

White always moves first. You can only move one of your pieces when it is your turn, except when you castle. To capture one of your opponent's pieces, you move your piece to a square occupied by one of your opponent's pieces. Your piece then occupies that square, and your opponent's piece is removed from the board. You are not allowed to move one of your pieces to a square already occupied by one of your own pieces. When a capture is possible, you can choose whether or not you want to make the capture. However, you may be forced to make a capture if it is necessary to save your king.

The Touch Move Rule

In tournament play, if you touch one of your pieces, you must move it. Once you let go of the piece, the move is over and can't be changed. When castling, always move your king first. If you should touch one of your opponent's pieces, you must capture it. If a move or capture cannot be made legally, there is no penalty. Players who wish to adjust a piece on the board must tell their opponent that they are not moving, only adjusting.

How Chessmen Move

The King. The king can move one square in any direction.

The Queen. The queen can move any number of squares horizontally, vertically, or diagonally if her path is not blocked.

The Rook. The rook can move any number of squares vertically or horizontally if its path is not blocked.

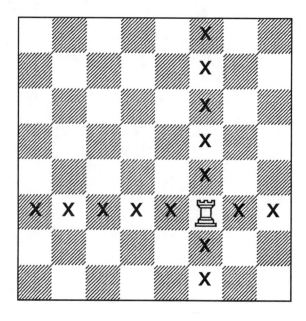

The Bishop. The bishop moves only diagonally any number of squares in either direction if its path is not blocked. Each player has one bishop that controls the light squares and another bishop that controls the dark squares.

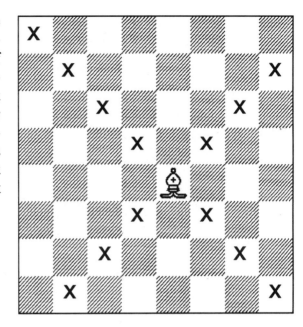

The Knight. The knight moves one square forward or backward and then two squares to either side, or one square to either side and then two squares forward or backward. These three squares form an "L". The knight is the only piece which may hop over any other pieces. The knight always stops on a square of a different color from which it started.

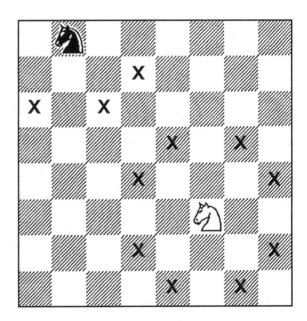

The Pawn. The pawn moves forward only, but it captures diagonally. Each pawn has the option to advance one or two squares the first time it moves. After that, it may move forward only one square per move. If a pawn advances all the way to the opposite end of the board, it must be promoted to a queen, rook, bishop, or knight of the same color, regardless of the number of such pieces already on the board.

En Passant Rule. En passant refers to a specific type of pawn capture. To capture en passant (in passing), the pawn which is to make the capture must be on its fifth rank, and the pawn which is to be captured must move two squares from its original rank on an adjacent file. The pawn on its fifth rank has the option on his next move only of capturing the pawn as if it had moved one square. If this option is not used on his next move, the option is lost.

Castling. Castling allows a player to move two of his pieces at once—his king and one of his rooks. A player has the option to castle once during a game. When you castle, you move the king two squares either to the right or to the left toward one of his rooks. The rook is then placed on the other side of the king in the square next to the king. The purpose of castling is to place your king in a safer position, and also to move your rook into a more active position.

There are certain restrictions for castling:

1) The pieces between the king and rook have been moved, and these squares are vacant.

2) Neither the king nor the rook have been previously moved.

3) The king must not be in check or pass through a square that is under attack.

Problem—En Passant Rule

Example:

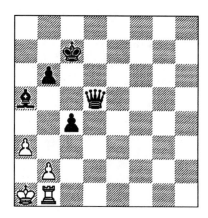

White to move.

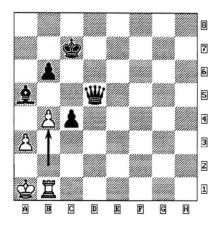

White moves b pawn two spaces.

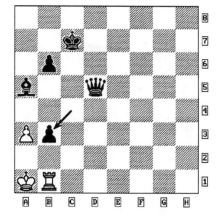

Black captures b pawn en passant.

10

Problem 1:

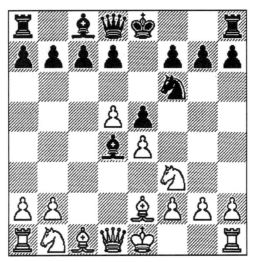

Black to move.

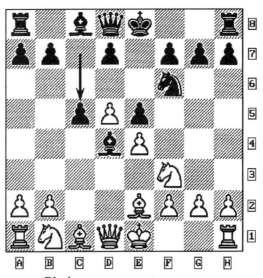

Black moves c pawn two spaces.

Can white capture black's c pawn?

See Answer—En Passant Rule, page 89

Problems—Castling

Example:
Black can castle either on the King-side or on the Queenside.

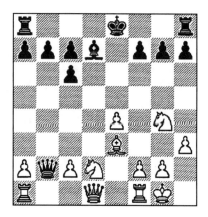

Black castles on the Kingside.

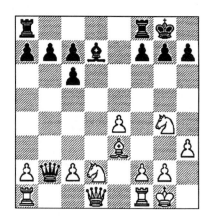

Black castles on the Queenside.

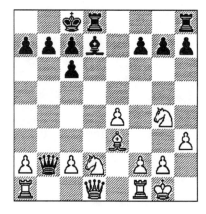

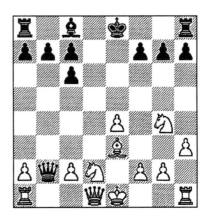

Problem 2:
White to move. Can white castle?

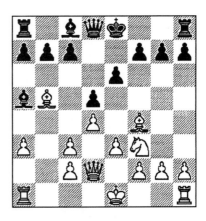

Problem 3:
Black to move. Can black castle?

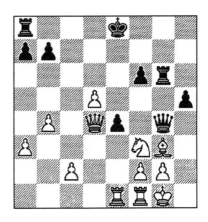

Problem 4:
Black to move. Can black castle?

See Answers—Castling, page 90

Problems—Perpetual Check

Example:

White to move. Black is close to winning the game, so white's queen keeps black's king in perpetual check in order for the game to end in a draw.

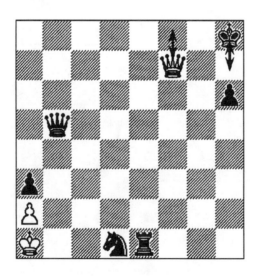

Problem 5:
Black to move. Can black keep white in perpetual check?

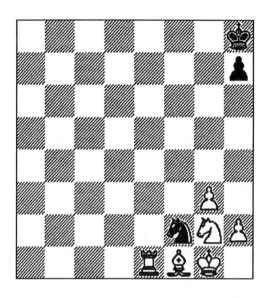

Problem 6:
Black to move. Can black keep white in perpetual check?

See Answers—Perpetual Check, page 92

CHAPTER 2

UNDERSTANDING THE VALUE OF CHESS PIECES AND PAWNS

Material Defined. The queen and rooks are called the "major pieces." The bishops and knights are called the "minor pieces." Although the term "pieces" is often used when referring to all the chessmen, it specifically refers to the major and minor pieces. Your pieces and pawns are known as your material.

Points of Value for Chess Pieces and Pawns

All chess pieces and pawns (except the king, which cannot be captured) have been given points of value based upon their fighting ability. The more powerful pieces have higher point values, because they can control more squares of the board.

Queen	9 points
Rook	5 points
Bishop	3 points
Knight	3 points
Pawn	1 point

Value For Value Rule

Don't give away a piece of greater value than the piece you will get in return, unless you will gain an advantage which justifies the sacrifice. Always apply the rule of value for value when capturing, exchanging, or threatening your opponent.

CHAPTER 3

THE BEGINNING OF A CHESS GAME—THE OPENING

Opening Objectives. The beginning of a chess game is referred to as the opening. At the beginning of a game, the queens, rooks, and bishops are completely blocked by pawns, making them powerless. In the opening moves, you must develop (bring out) your minor and major pieces to their best fighting positions. Development is complete when the first rank has been cleared of all pieces except the king and rooks, and the king has been castled to a safe position.

Strategy for Good Development

Fight to Control the Center Area of the Board. Each player brings out his pieces as fast as possible and fights for positions on the board which give his pieces the most control of the board, in other words, positions which give his pieces the best mobility. You especially want to control the "four center squares" of the board. The following diagram indicates the center area of the board:

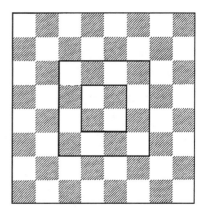

Development. To gain control of the center, you usually develop one or two central pawns, a knight, a bishop or knight, then you free your other bishop.

The First Move. For inexperienced players, a good first move would be to move the pawn in front of the king two squares. The pawn occupies one of the four center squares, and this move opens up diagonal moves for both the queen and bishop. If the player has the black pieces, and his opponent starts with either his king's or queen's pawn, a good counter move would be to move the corresponding pawn forward two spaces in order to prevent his opponent's pawn from moving further ahead.

The Importance of Pawns. Pawn play is a very important part of chess. The pawn does not seem very powerful, but if it reaches the opposite end of the board, it is promoted to a higher rank. Since pawns can become powerful, they should always be protected. Avoid making too many pawn moves early in the game. Keep in mind that pawns can only move forward—they cannot retreat.

Developing Your Knights. A good position for a knight is one that would control one of the four center squares. A knight is a short-range fighter, and it is much more powerful when placed in the center. Avoid posting a knight on the edge of the board, as its moves are much more limited there. In the following diagram, knights are controlling the center squares:

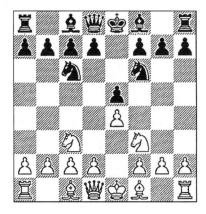

The Weakest Square in the Opening. The weakest square in the opening for each player is the square in front of his king's bishop, as this square is guarded only by the king. It is important to protect this weak square.

black's weak opening square ——————

white's weak opening square ——————

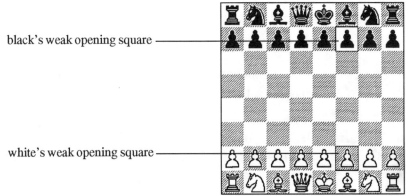

20

Developing Your Bishops. Since the position for a bishop depends on your opponent's game plan, the knight is usually developed first. One possible development for a bishop is to attack your opponent's weak square, as shown in the diagram:

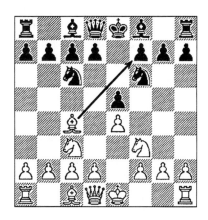

Fianchettoed Bishops. Another possible development for a bishop is to move the pawn in front of your knight up one square, and then move your bishop to the square formerly occupied by that pawn. This is referred to as "fianchettoing" a bishop. The bishop is a long-range fighter and can control the center from a distance. In the following diagram, both bishops are fianchettoed:

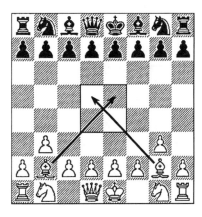

Developing Your Queen. Bringing your queen into play too early in the game is not a good idea. You may have to make several early moves defending your queen instead of developing your pieces and planning an attack. After two or three minor pieces have been developed, the queen is often developed to back up the center or other pieces. In the early stages of the game, the queen does not ordinarily occupy squares in the exact center—her power is directed towards the center. The queen is often moved to the second rank or sometimes to the third rank to one of the positions shown in the diagram:

Developing Your Rooks. After castling, the rooks are usually moved to the center files on the first rank. Generally, rooks should be placed on open or half-open files. An

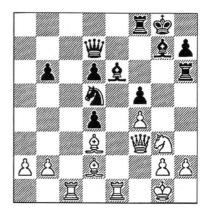

open file has no pawns on it; a half-open file has a pawn of only one color on it. Rooks operate best on open files, because they can penetrate the enemy position. If a rook can reach the 7th or 8th rank, it can attack many pawns and often trap the enemy king on the back rank. In the following diagram, white's rooks are controlling open files and threaten to invade enemy territory for better positions:

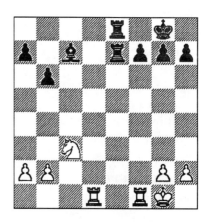

Doubling Rooks on an Open File. A player often doubles his rooks on an open file in order to control it. To double your rooks, you advance one rook one square on the file, and then bring the other rook behind it as shown in the diagram:

Back-rank Mate. The rook has the ability to checkmate the king on the last rank when the opposing king is imprisoned by his own pawns. This is referred to as back-rank mate, and is shown in the diagram:

Additional Guidelines for the Opening

Even Development. You should develop both sides of the board as evenly as possible.

Avoid Moving a Piece Twice. You should not move a piece twice during the opening, unless it is under attack. If your piece controls any of the four center squares and it is not in danger, bring up other pieces to control more of the center squares. Any unnecessary moves which do not promote the development of your own pieces, or which do not interfere with your opponent's development, are a waste of time.

Protect Each Piece. Try to protect each piece as soon as possible. This creates a strong defense. None of your pieces can be taken without a loss to your opponent.

Capturing Stray Pawns. It is not always wise to capture stray pawns in the opening. Such a capture may cost you valuable time, which should have been used for developing your pieces. In some chess openings, called gambits, a pawn or even a piece is sacrificed as part of a plan for an early attack. If you waste too much time on the gain of material and neglect your development, the gambit player often succeeds with his attack.

Make Good Developing Moves. Always try to make good developing moves. Let your opponent be the first to neglect his development.

Understanding Tempo. If a player places one of his pieces in a position in which it may be driven to a bad square by one of his opponent's attacking pieces, and the attacking piece then occupies a good square, then the attacking piece has won time or "tempo." After the player's retreat, it is again his opponent's move. His opponent has gained the initiative. When choosing each move, think ahead to determine whether or not your opponent can attack and force your piece to a bad position.

Do Not Attack Prematurely. Study the weaknesses in your opponent's game structure. Once you find a vulnerable target, make sure your attack is well planned.

Castle Early in the Game. The purpose of castling is to place your king in a safer position, and to move your rook into a more active position.

CHAPTER 4

STALEMATE AND CHECKMATE

Stalemate. When a king "is not in check," but the only possible move on the board would put him in check, then the king is stalemated. When stalemate occurs, the game ends in a draw. When trying to checkmate your opponent's king, be careful of any moves that will result in stalemate.

Checkmate. When a king "is in check" and only has moves that will put him in check, then the king is checkmated. When checkmate occurs, the game is over.

Checkmating the Enemy King

Queen and King Against King. The queen and king must drive the enemy king to the edge or corner of the board.

Rook and King Against King. The rook and king must drive the enemy king to the edge of the board.

Two Bishops and King Against King. The bishops and king must drive the enemy king into one of the corners of the board.

King, Bishop, and Knight Against King. The enemy king must be driven into the same color corner as the bishop. The king and knight must block the enemy king's other escape squares.

King and One Pawn Against King. Unless your pawn can reach the 8th rank untouched, you must use your king as its escort.

Two Rooks Against King. The two rooks must drive the king to the edge of the board.

Queen and Knight Against King. The queen and knight should drive the king to the edge of the board.

Queen and Bishop Against King.
The queen and bishop must drive the king to the edge or corner of the board.

Bad Combinations for Checkmate. The following combinations will probably end in a draw:

- When each player has king and one bishop left on the board, and the bishops move on squares of different colors.

- King and bishop against king.

- King and knight against king.

- King and two knights against king.

Problems—Stalemate

Example: Black to move. The black king has no move that does not put him in check, therefore it is stalemate.

Problem 7:
Black to move. Is this stalemate?

Problem 8:
White to move. Is this stalemate?

Problem 9:
White to move. Is this stalemate?

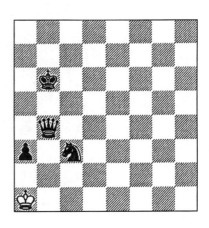

Problem 10:
White to move. Is this stalemate?

Problem 11:
Black to move. Is this stalemate?

See Answers--Stalemate, page 94

CHAPTER 5

ATTACKING TECHNIQUES

The Pin. The pin is an attack on a piece which cannot move away, because if it moves, a more valuable piece will be attacked. When a player is pinned, he should try to counter attack against the attacking piece or look for the possibility to make a similar pin against his opponent's pieces.

Breaking Pins. As a general rule, a player should learn to break pins immediately. The reason for this is that the square on which the pinned piece is attacked is a weakness which will be a target for additional attacks. Your opponent can continue to attack the pinned piece in an effort to destroy your position.

Examples of Pins:

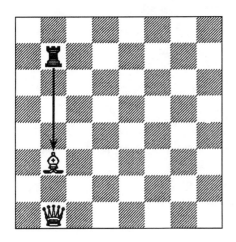 

The Fork. A fork is an attack on two or more pieces.

Examples of Forks:

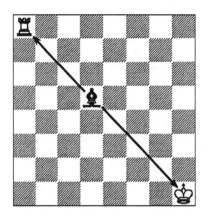
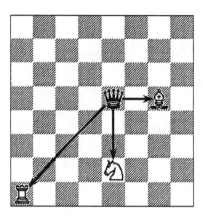

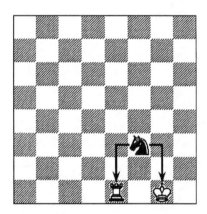

Planning An Attack

When planning an attack, look for unguarded pieces or inadequately guarded pieces. If you find an inadequately guarded piece, determine whether the guard can be driven off, captured, or weakened. Look for overburdened pieces. Is it possible to attack a piece that has an important defensive function? A well planned attack involves coordinating your pieces and bringing them into position before beginning your attack.

Problems—Pins

Example: White to move. Black's queen has pinned white's f pawn to the king. White cannot take black's bishop on e3, which is attacking white's rook on c1.

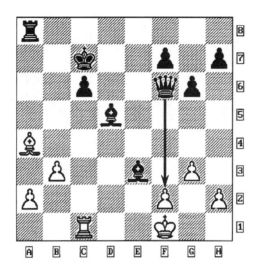

Problem 12: White to move. Black has forked white's rook and knight. Look for a pin that will prevent black from winning one of white's pieces.

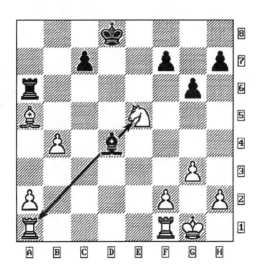

Problem 13: Black to move. Look for the pin.

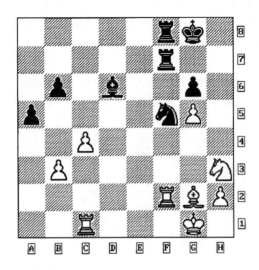

Problem 14: White to move. Look for the move that takes advantage of a pin which already exists.

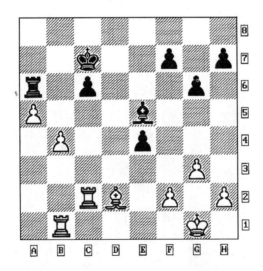

See Answers—Pins, page 96

Problems—Forks

Example: White to move. Black's queen is attacking white's king and rook. Since white is in check, he must move his king. White's king cannot take black's queen, as it is protected by black's bishop on d4.

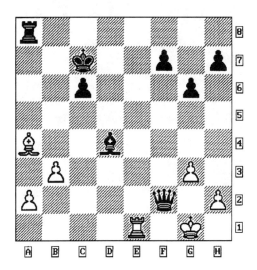

Problem 15: Black to move. Look for the move that will fork two of white's pieces.

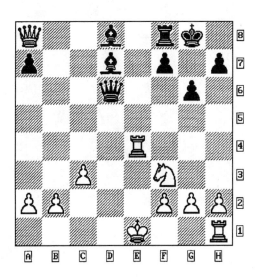

Problem 16: White to move. Look for a forking move using one of the knights.

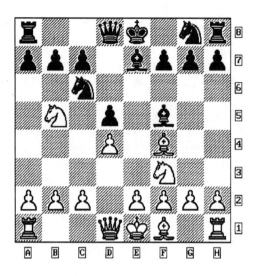

Problem 17: Black to move. Look for a powerful forking move.

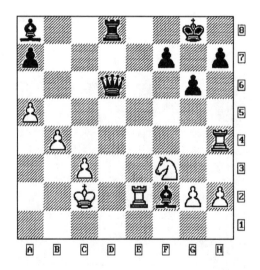

See Answers—Forks, page 98

CHAPTER 6

MAKING THE BEST MOVE

Threats and Potential Threats. Before you make your move, review your opponent's threats. Ask yourself the following questions:

- If your opponent has attacked one of your pieces, can you defend it or counterattack?

- If your opponent's last move has allowed you to make a capture or exchange, will it be to his advantage?

- If you make a capture or exchange, will it give your opponent a better position or create a weakness for you?

- How will your opponent respond to the move you are going to make? It is important to anticipate your opponent's threats.

Mobility. You want to control as much of the board as possible, so that your pieces will be able to travel where they are needed. Helpful guidelines for mobility are:

- Avoid moves which cause your pieces to interfere with each other.

- Try to pick the move that will not block the path of one of your other pieces, or cause it to be trapped with no escape route.

- Choose moves that will provide you with good mobility and restrict your opponent's mobility.

Pressure Your Opponent. When you have a choice of acceptable moves, choose a move which creates difficulties for your opponent. This will limit your opponent's choice of moves.

Watch the Board. Don't become so involved in your own game that you lose sight of what your opponent is doing. Always watch the entire board, and look carefully every time your opponent moves.

Take Your Time. Take the time to carefully study your opponent's last move, and to carefully plan your next move. Never rush yourself, as this could cause you to make a careless mistake. Studying your opponent's game and planning your next move takes time.

Exchanging Pieces. The following guidelines will be helpful when faced with the decision of trading pieces:

- If you are controlling the game, and your pieces are better developed than your opponent's, try not to exchange pieces, unless it gives you a definite advantage.

- Do not trade pieces when your opponent's pieces are in cramped positions.

- It may be to your advantage to exchange pieces, if it will weaken your opponent's pawn structure.

- If you are ahead in material, you might want to trade a couple pieces in order to simplify the game.

- It may be necessary to make an exchange in order to control or open a file.

- It might be necessary to make an exchange in order to eliminate a defender or attacker.

- It might be necessary to exchange in order not to lose time by retreating. An attacking piece may win time or tempo if your piece can be driven to a bad square, and the attacking piece then occupies a good square. If you have the choice of retreating a piece with loss of tempo or exchanging it for an enemy piece, you should choose to make the exchange.

Defensive Strategy. Defensive strategy is an important part of your game. Some helpful guidelines for defense are:

- As a rule, you should not use your pieces strictly for defense. Pawns make the best defenders.

- When you are attacked, look for the possibility of a counterattack. Is your opponent's attack weak or premature?

- If your position is basically defensive, exchange as much as possible. It is usually to your advantage to exchange a passive piece for an active or attacking enemy piece.

CHAPTER 7

OPEN AND CLOSED GAMES

Open Games. An open game refers to a game where the center pawns are exchanged, and the pieces are able to move through the center.

- This diagram illustrates an open game:

- Files d and e are open files (files with no pawns on them), and file c is a half-open file (a file with a pawn of only one color on it).

- Having no pawns in the center also opens up the diagonals in the center of the board.

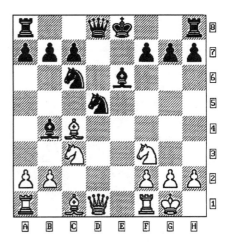

Some valuable tips for open games are:

- Castle early. If the center is open, you must safeguard your king.

- Develop your pieces quickly. In open games, you must find good fighting positions as soon as possible to protect your territory and aggressively attack your opponent.

- Bishops are much more active and therefore more valuable in open positions than they are in closed positions.

Closed Games. A closed game refers to a game where the pawns block the center. This interferes with the pieces' ability to move in the center.

- This diagram illustrates a closed game:

- The center of the board is completely blocked by pawns.

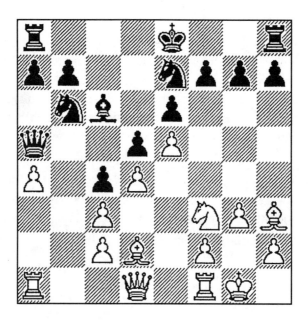

Some valuable tips for closed games are:

- If the center is blocked, it is not necessary to castle early.

- Bishops tend to become inactive in closed games; whereas knights are not restricted by a closed center. For this reason, your knights may be more valuable than your bishops.

- If your position is too cramped, it may be necessary to open up your game by making exchanges.

- If you are behind in development, try to keep the game closed.

King-pawn Openings and Queen-pawn Openings. King-pawn openings usually lead to open positions, and queen-pawn openings usually lead to closed positions. The big difference in these two openings is the ability to advance both center pawns two squares each.

- King-pawn Openings. After opening with the king-pawn two squares, white will soon be able to move the queen-pawn two squares, because the queen-pawn is already protected by the queen.

- Queen-pawn Openings. When white opens by moving the queen-pawn two squares, he usually has to prepare the king-pawn advance of two squares very carefully. This creates a slower game. If black's first move doesn't challenge the king-pawn's advancement square, white can usually advance his king-pawn two squares right away.

Your First Move. If you are still opening all of your games by moving the king-pawn two squares, you should now play several games opening with the queen-pawn advancing two squares. You will discover that your games will be quite different.

CHAPTER 8

UNDERSTANDING PAWNS AND PAWN STRUCTURE

Understanding pawn structure will be of great benefit when planning your strategy. It is important to be able to:

- Understand the meaning of weak squares.

- Understand over-protection.

- Understand the pawn's role in protecting the castled king.

- Identify weak pawns.

- Understand the importance of blockading a passed pawn.

- Understand pawn chains and how to attack them.

Weak Squares

A weak square is one that lacks good protection and gives your opponent a target for an invasion or attack. Avoid creating holes (weak squares) in your pawn structure that could be occupied by one of your opponent's pieces.

Over-protection

In addition to protecting your pieces, pawns, and weak squares, it is necessary to protect important squares as well. Over-protection means to provide defense beyond the threat of attack. Over-protection applies to important center squares, strong blockading squares, strong passed pawns, and the base of a pawn chain. Ordinary weak squares should not be over-protected.

Pawn Structure and the Castled King

After castling, the three pawns in front of the king, referred to as the wing pawns, become the king's shield. Moving any of these pawns in the beginning of the game will create weak squares near the castled king. For this reason the wing pawns should not be moved early in the game unless there is a good reason, such as a fianchettoed bishop or driving away an enemy piece. A knight can be used to strengthen this position by protecting the pawn on the far right, as shown in the diagram:

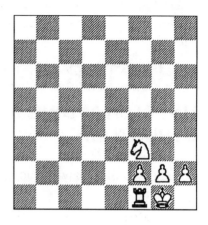

The pawn formation in the following diagram creates weak squares near the king and opens a direct line to the king:

The fianchettoed bishop is a good formation, as long as the bishop remains in place. If the bishop is moved, do not let an enemy piece occupy the hole in your pawn structure.

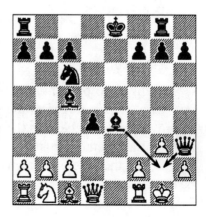

46

Weak Pawns

Weak Pawn Defined. A weak pawn is a target for an attack and the player must use one of his pieces to defend the pawn. Weak pawns include:

1) Isolated Pawns. An isolated pawn, one with no pawn neighbors, is a weakness because it cannot be guarded by another pawn.

- If you have an isolated pawn, you should guard against having it blocked, and look for the possibility of trading it for a good enemy pawn.

- If you are playing against an isolated pawn, you should restrict it's advance by controlling or occupying the square in front of it, attack it, or look for the opportunity to exchange pieces to intensify its weakness.

- Note the difference between an isolated pawn and a passed pawn. An isolated pawn is always restrained or blocked by at least one enemy pawn. A passed pawn has passed all enemy pawns capable of capturing it.

This diagram illustrates an isolated pawn:

This diagram illustrates a passed pawn:

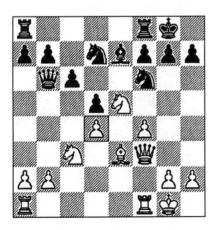
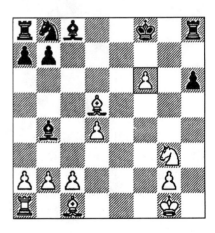

2) Doubled Pawns. Doubled pawns are two pawns of the same color lined up on the same file. Doubled pawns cannot protect each other, and they tend to advance slowly.

● The worst kinds of doubled pawns are isolated ones, where neither of the two pawns can be protected by another pawn. These pawns can be easily blocked by an enemy piece.

● Doubled pawns can be an advantage if you can control the open lines that will be created, or if one or both of the doubled pawns control important squares.

● If you have doubled pawns, you should avoid moving them unless you have to move them or you can make a good exchange. You should use your rooks, or some of your other pieces, to control the open files.

● If you are playing against doubled pawns, you should restrain their movement, avoid exchanges that will improve your opponent's pawn structure, and attack the weak pawns and weak square(s).

This diagram illustrates doubled pawns:

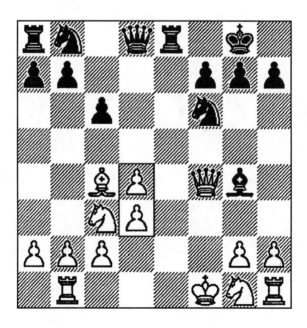

3) Backward Pawns. A backward pawn is a pawn that has been left behind without the protection of other pawns.

- A backward pawn's weakness or strength depends on if it is on an open file, how well it is defended, how well the square directly in front of it is defended, and how well it defends the pawns that have gone on ahead of it.

- A backward pawn on an open file is a target for attacks.

This diagram illustrates a backward pawn:

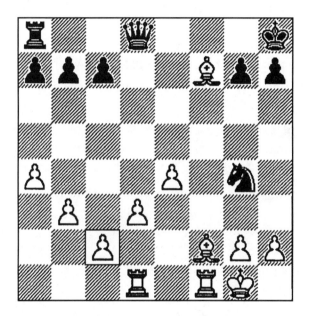

Blockade

Blockade refers to the immobilizing of an enemy passed pawn (a pawn that has passed by all enemy pawns capable of capturing it) by placing a piece directly in front of it.

- The blockading square is usually an important square, and should be well protected.

- The best blockader is a knight, because of its ability to jump over pieces.

- The minor pieces, knights and bishops, can keep their positions under an attack. The king or queen would not be the best choice for a blockader, as they could be forced to leave their positions under an attack.

- Once a player has blockaded a passed pawn, he should create a strong blockade by bringing up other pieces to backup and defend the blockader.

- If the player has a strong blockade, the blockader may be able to attack another piece and return to a blockading position, or a different piece will be in a position to become the blockader.

- A blockader that is poorly protected will be driven off or captured, and the passed pawn will continue to advance.

This diagram illustrates a blockade:

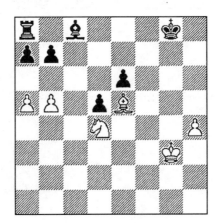

Passed Pawns

A passed pawn is a pawn that has passed by all enemy pawns capable of capturing it. A passed pawn is a potential threat which cannot be ignored! The closer it gets to the 8th rank, the more dangerous it becomes. It is absolutely necessary to block the progress of a passed pawn. When a piece is used to blockade the pawn, it has the advantage of being able to use the pawn as a shield. If a passed pawn cannot be restrained, it should be captured. Once a passed pawn is created, the player must make it worthwhile. You don't want a passed pawn if it can be blockaded, unless you have play elsewhere and the passed pawn will be an advantage in the end game.

A passed pawn should advance when:

● The pawn can get nearer to its goal.

● The pawn will protect important squares.

● The advancing pawn opens moves or positions for another piece.

● The pawn is used as a sacrifice.

Pawn Chains

A pawn chain is two or more pawns of the same color linked diagonally. The base of a pawn chain is its weakest point, because it is not guarded by another pawn.

● This diagram illustrates a pawn chain:

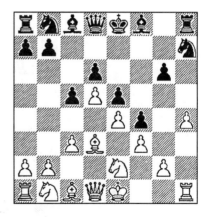

- In the middle game, the purpose of attacking the pawn base is to create a new weakness elsewhere on the board. When a new weakness has been successfully created, the base is released, and the new weakness is attacked.

- In the end game, the purpose of attacking the pawn base is to conquer it. Once the base is destroyed, the remaining pawns are weakened.

CHAPTER 9

UNDERSTANDING KNIGHTS AND BISHOPS

Understanding the Knight

Knights need good fighting positions. When choosing a position for your knight, keep in mind the following information:

- A knight is more effective when it is far into enemy territory.

- The knight must work together with other pieces and pawns.

- The knight must be in a useful area of the board.

- If a good position for your knight exists, pursue it.

- If a good position does not exist, try to create one.

Using the Knight's Special Fighting Abilities. The following information will give you a better understanding of how to use your knights effectively:

- Knights are very useful in closed positions.

- Knights can be very valuable in open positions, if they have good fighting positions.

- Knights in your territory are defensive.

- Knights in enemy territory can find good attacking positions.

- Avoid creating weak squares deep in your territory which would create a good attacking position for an enemy knight.

- Knights are usually superior to bishops in games ending with pawns on only one side of the board. This is due to their ability to go to either color.

- Knights are the best blockaders of passed pawns.

Understanding the Bishop

Bishops are long-range fighters that can only travel on the diagonals. The following information will give you a better understanding of bishops:

- In the middle game, when players have bishops of opposite colors, one bishop can attack a point that the other cannot defend. This can be an advantage.

- Bishops are usually strongest in open positions.

- Side by side, two bishops are very powerful.

- When you have two bishops, open up the position.

- In the middle game, you should try to restrict the enemy bishop by putting your pawns on the bishop's color. The pawns should be well defended, which will make them relatively safe.

- In the end game, your pawns should be on the opposite color of the opposing bishop. This prevents the bishop from attacking them.

- In the end game, with passed pawns on both sides of the board, bishops are stronger than knights, because of their long-range abilities.

Bishops Vs. Knights

The Value of Bishops and Knights. At the beginning of a game, bishops and knights are given a value of 3 points. But because their fighting abilities and maneuverability are so different, the positions of these pieces and the pawn structure in each individual game will determine which bishops and knights are more valuable.

The Fight for Superiority. Determining which bishops and knights will be superior during the game sets the stage for a battle between bishops and knights. The following guidelines will help you with your battle of bishops vs. knights:

- Two bishops are superior over two knights. The reason for this is that two bishops can work together as a team, whereas two knights do not work well as a team.

- If you have two knights vs. your opponent's two bishops, one of the following should apply: a) You need a blocked position and good fighting positions for your knights, or b) You should trade one of your knights for one of your opponent's bishops. This will give you a more favorable knight vs. bishop situation.

- If you have a bishop and knight vs. two bishops situation, you should exchange your bishop for one of your opponent's bishops.

CHAPTER 10

MIDDLE AND END GAME STRATEGY

Middle Game Objectives. In the middle game, you must combine the capture of enemy pieces with a strategy to eventually attack the enemy king or queen.

- Your attacking pieces should be in good fighting positions, and your pawns should create a strong formation to prevent enemy attack and invasion.

- Your pieces and pawns should work together to defend your king and your territory.

- Always strive to increase the mobility of your pieces, and to reduce your opponent's terrain.

Opening Lines and Controlling the Board. It is important to control as much of the board as possible without creating serious weaknesses. The following guidelines will help you in the middle game:

- Learn to control open files and diagonals so that your pieces can travel where they are needed.

- Learn to exchange pawns to open lines for your pieces. This will increase your attacking chances in a chosen area of the board, and better mobility of your pieces will make it easier for you to plan your strategy.

- Avoid too many pawn exchanges. Keep the files and diagonals closed in the areas in which your opponent threatens to attack, and avoid creating pawn weaknesses and open lines in the king's castled position.

Material Advantage and Checkmate. In the middle game, a player uses one of the following strategies:

1) Strategy for a material advantage:

- Gain a material advantage, and then trade some of your extra material for your opponent's remaining pieces.

- Use your remaining material to capture your opponent's pawns.

- Advance your pawns to the 8th rank to be promoted.

- Checkmate your opponent's king.

2) Strategy to checkmate the enemy king:

- Study the position of your opponent's king and look for a weak square in the king's defense. The weak square is not always located near the king.

- After finding or creating a weak square, plan your attack on the enemy king.

- Close in on the king with as many pieces as possible.

- A knight posted near the enemy king is always ready to work with your other pieces in a strong attack.

- Keep the king in check with every move until you have checkmate.

END GAME STRATEGY

End Game Objectives. In the end game, not too many pieces and pawns are left on the board. The promotion of a passed pawn or pawns is often the strategy used to checkmate the enemy king.

Guidelines for the End Game. Some guidelines for the end game are as follows:

- As a general rule, the player with the material advantage tries to exchange queens in order to simplify the game.

- Bring your king towards the center or to his most active position. Since there are fewer pieces on the board in the end game, the king joins the fight. It is especially important for the king to fight against any passed pawns.

- Put your pieces on their most active squares and coordinate them with a plan in mind.

- Concentrate on your opponent's weaknesses.

- Attack your opponent's pawns.

- Create one or more passed pawns, and advance your pawns until they are promoted, or until your opponent sacrifices a piece for one of them.

Part 2
Reference Section

HOW TO READ AND WRITE CHESS

Chess notation is used to record each move of the game. Knowing how to use notation enables the chess player to record and replay his or her own games, as well as replay and study games of other players.

Algebraic Notation

Algebraic notation is the most commonly used by today's players. Each square is identified by its file and its rank.

- Files are the vertical rows labeled a-h.

- Ranks are the horizontal rows numbered 1-8.

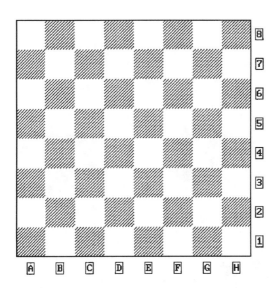

The chess pieces are abbreviated as follows:

K = King	Q = Queen	R = Rook	B = Bishop
N = Knight	P = Pawn (the pawn is often not given a letter).		

Other algebraic notations include:

x = capture	+ = check	mate = checkmate
e.p. = en passant	0-0 = kingside castling	! = good move
? = bad move	0-0-0 = queenside castling	

When a piece is moved, give the letter for the piece, then the file and rank of the square it moved to. When a pawn is moved, only the name of the square it moved to is usually given.

Example: 1.e4   e5
        2.Nf3   Nc6
        3.Bc4   Bc5

When a pawn makes a capture, name the file the pawn moved from, and name the square the piece is captured on.

Example: exf5

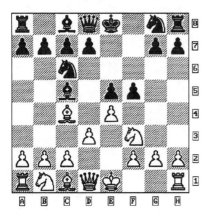

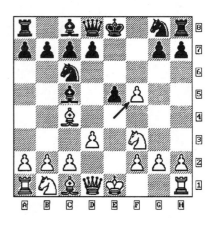

64

When a pawn makes a capture en passant, name the file the pawn moved from, identify the square where the pawn was captured, and follow this information with the letters "e.p."

Example: 27. f5 g5
28. fxg6 e.p.

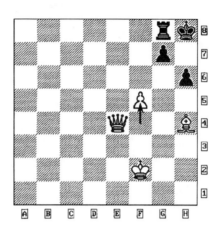

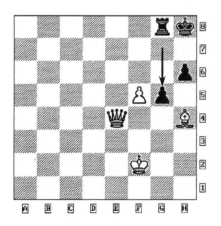

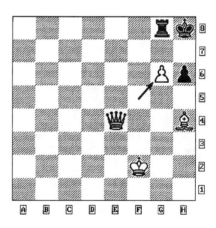

If it is possible for two of the same pieces of the same color to move to the same square, you name the file that the piece moved from and then identify the square it moved to. If using the file doesn't work, use the rank instead.

Example: 24. Rhxd5 Ra6
25. R1d3

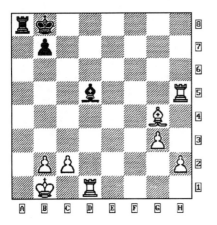

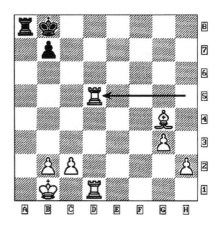

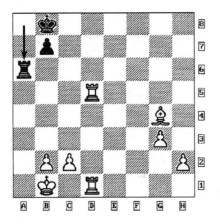

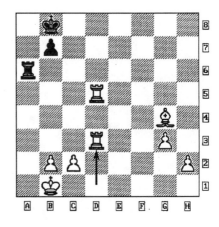

When promoting a pawn, the pawn is exchanged for a queen, rook, bishop or knight. Identify the promoted pawn when recording the move.

Example: 27 ...e1Q

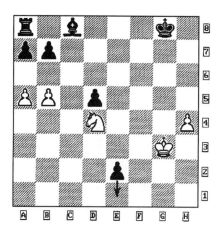 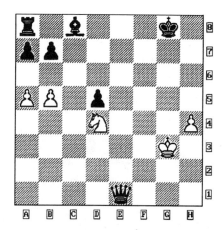

Descriptive Notation

Descriptive notation is an older form of chess notation, and it is still used in many of the chess books. In descriptive notation:

● Ranks are numbered from 1 (the rank closest to each player) to 8 (the rank furthest from each player). Therefore white's 1st rank is black's 8th rank.

● Files are named by the piece (on the first rank) that occupies that file at the beginning of the game.

● The chessboard is divided into the queen's side and the king's side. All the pieces on the queen's side are referred to as the queen's pieces, and all the pieces on the king's side are referred to as the king's pieces.

Algebraic files:		Descriptive files:
a file	=	the Queen-Rook file
b file	=	the Queen-Knight file
c file	=	the Queen-Bishop file
d file	=	the Queen file
e file	=	the King File
f file	=	the King-Bishop file
g file	=	the King-Knight file
h file	=	the King-Rook file

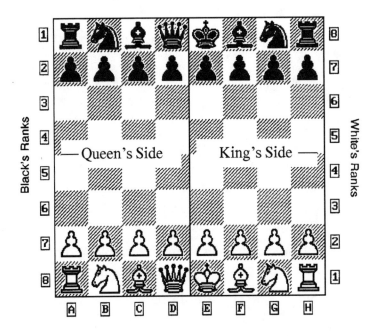

The pieces are abbreviated as follows:

K = King	Q = Queen	R = Rook
B = Bishop	N = Knight	P = Pawn

The additional letter (Q or K) is used in descriptive notation whenever necessary.

QR	=	Queen's Rook	KR	=	King's Rook
QN	=	Queen's Knight	KN	=	King's Knight
QB	=	Queen's Bishop	KB	=	King's Bishop
QRP	=	Queen's Rook Pawn	KRP	=	King's Rook Pawn
QNP	=	Queen's Knight Pawn	KNP	=	King's Knight Pawn
QBP	=	Queen's Bishop Pawn	KBP	=	King's Bishop Pawn
QP	=	Queen's Pawn	KP	=	King's Pawn

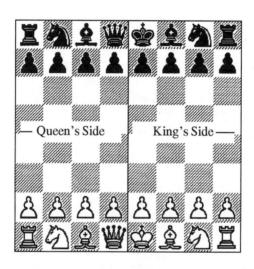

Other descriptive notations include:

—	=	moved to	?	=	bad move
ch	=	check	e.p.	=	en passant
!	=	good move	O-O	=	kingside castling
x	=	capture	O-O-O	=	queenside castling
mate	=	checkmate			

When a pawn is promoted, it is shown by a parentheses sign ( ). For example P-KB8 (Q).

Each square of the chessboard is identified by the file and rank as follows:

White records his moves according to this diagram:

QR8	QN8	QB8	Q8	K8	KB8	KN8	KR8
QR7	QN7	QB7	Q7	K7	KB7	KN7	KR7
QR6	QN6	QB6	Q6	K6	KB6	KN6	KR6
QR5	QN5	QB5	Q5	K5	KB5	KN5	KR5
QR4	QN4	QB4	Q4	K4	KB4	KN4	KR4
QR3	QN3	QB3	Q3	K3	KB3	KN3	KR3
QR2	QN2	QB2	Q2	K2	KB2	KN2	KR2
QR1	QN1	QB1	Q1	K1	KB1	KN1	KR1

Black records his moves according to this diagram:

QR1	QN1	QB1	Q1	K1	KB1	KN1	KR1
QR2	QN2	QB2	Q2	K2	KB2	KN2	KR2
QR3	QN3	QB3	Q3	K3	KB3	KN3	KR3
QR4	QN4	QB4	Q4	K4	KB4	KN4	KR4
QR5	QN5	QB5	Q5	K5	KB5	KN5	KR5
QR6	QN6	QB6	Q6	K6	KB6	KN6	KR6
QR7	QN7	QB7	Q7	K7	KB7	KN7	KR7
QR8	QN8	QB8	Q8	K8	KB8	KN8	KR8

When a piece is moved, give the letter for the piece. Unlike algebraic, the pawn is always identified. The squares are identified by descriptive file and rank.

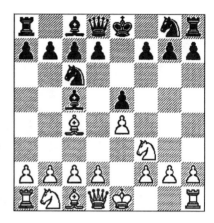

Example:

1. P-K4   P-K4
2. N-KB3   N-QB3
3. B-B4   B-B4

It is not necessary to identify the square as QB4, as only one bishop can move to a B4 square.

When a capture is made, the piece moved and the captured piece are identified.

Example: P x P

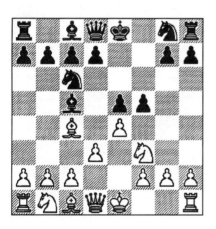

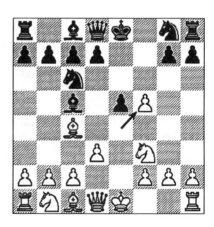

If more than one pawn capture was possible, the pawns would need to be identified such as: KP x BP.

When a pawn makes a capture en passant, "e.p." is written after the move.

Example:

27. P-B5 P-N4
28. P x P e.p.

If it is possible for two of the same pieces of the same color to move to the same square, you name the file that the piece moved from. If using the file doesn't work, use the rank instead.

Example:

24. R/R x B   R-R3
25. R/1-Q3

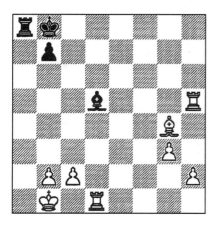

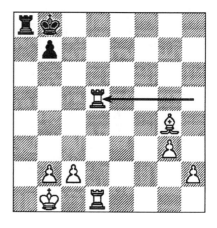

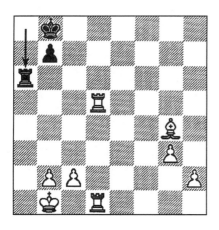

When promoting a pawn, the pawn is exchanged for a queen, rook, bishop or knight. Identify the promoted pawn when recording the move.

Example: 27 ...P-K8(Q)

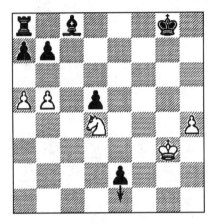 

FOOL'S MATE AND SCHOLAR'S MATE

Fool's Mate. Fool's mate is the simplest of all checkmates, being accomplished in two moves as follows:

1. g4 e5
2. f4 Qh4, mate.

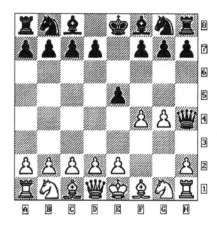

Scholar's Mate. Another checkmate to be aware of is scholar's mate, which is shown as follows:

1. e4 e5
2. Bc4 Bc5
3. Qh5 d6
4. Qxf7, mate.

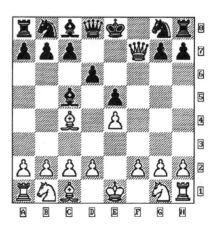

THE CHESS CLOCK

When most people first learn chess, they play without a clock. However, some chess games have time controls. Each player must make a certain number of moves in a certain amount of time. The player who does not make the required number of moves in the specified time forfeits the game. A chess clock actually holds two clocks. Each clock is set separately, and there is a button over each clock. When one button is pushed down, the clock below it stops and the other clock starts. Pressing down both buttons halfway stops both clocks.

A chess clock is set to the side of the board, between the two players. The player using the black pieces chooses which side of the board the clock is placed on. The clocks are always set so that the time allowed expires at 6 o'clock. An extra minute is always allowed in case there are flaws in the clock. When White is ready to start, Black presses the button over his or her clock. This starts White's clock. White makes a move and presses the button over his clock, etc. When a player's flag falls at 6 o'clock, he or she must have made at least the number of moves specified. Otherwise the player loses on time. Chess notation is required in order to keep track of the number of moves.

Time Controls

There are two kinds of time controls. In the first kind of time control, each player must make a certain number of moves in a given amount of time. The second kind of time control is referred to as a Sudden Death time control. In Sudden Death, the game is over when a player exceeds the time limit. The player exceeding the time limit first loses the game.

In some tournaments, two time controls are given. Time controls of 40/2, 30/1 means that each player has 2 hours for the first 40 moves and one hour for an additional 30 moves.

Time controls not in full hours are stated in minutes. Time controls of 40/90, 20/30 means that each player has 90 minutes to complete the first 40 moves, then 30 minutes for an additional 20 moves.

Any time that a player has not used at the end of the first session is carried over to the second session. If time controls are 40/90, 20/30 and White uses only 60 minutes for his first 40 moves, he gets to carry over the 30 minutes he has not used into the second time control, giving him one hour for the next 20 moves.

A sudden-death time control of 30 minutes is stated as "game/30" or "G/30." Sudden-death time limits can also be used as a secondary time control. This type of sudden-death time control is written "SD/30."

A time control of 40/90, SD/30 means that each player has 90 minutes for the first 40 moves, and 30 minutes to complete the game.

Speed Chess

Speed chess refers to games played with a very fast time limit, often allowing each player only five minutes to make all his or her moves. Speed chess may be fun and beneficial for advanced players, but not for beginners. Speed chess tends to promote superficial thinking. Beginners need to learn to take their time to think and study the board. Speed chess can cause beginners to rush their moves and make careless mistakes in all their games. This can be very frustrating and discouraging.

THE CHESS LADDER

Grade(s) _____

Each player will play _____ matches. After each match, each player will record W (win), L (loss) or D (draw); and the # of your opponent. The ladder will be played in three phases:

- _____ games...Challenge a player with the same number of wins and losses as your own.

- _____ games...Challenge any player.

- _____ games...Players at the top of the ladder must play for 1st and 2nd place.

Player's # and Name	Round 1	Round 2	Round 3	Round 4	Totals W - L - D
0 Example	W 5	L 3	D 1	W 2	2 - 1 - 1

CHESS BOOKS FOR IMPROVING YOUR GAME

Motivated by my son's enthusiasm for chess, I purchased and studied several different chess books. My purpose for writing A SIMPLE GUIDE TO CHESS, was to take the struggle out of learning chess, and bring chess to an understandable level for beginners of all ages. In my opinion, all of these books will be very helpful to players who want to improve their game. (Most of these books can be purchased through the U.S. Chess Federation.)

SCHOOLS:

- Schools should have *School Mates* and a variety of books on chess in their library for enthusiastic students. Enthusiastic students will learn on their own, and other students will learn from them.

Beginners:

For beginners, especially those in the elementary grades, it is important to let them play chess often, with some instruction and chess problems to help them improve their games. For this I recommend the following:

- *School Mates*—This is the U.S. Chess Federation magazine for beginners. It includes instructional articles and chess problems. School Mates also lists all official U.S. Chess Federation tournaments, both national events and state events.

Advanced Beginners:

Since control of the center is so important, most beginners are taught to open with either the King-pawn or the Queen-pawn. After a while, advanced beginners can feel frustrated when their game seems to be stuck in the same old rut, and they don't know what to do about it. Understanding more about opening moves for the King-pawn or Queen-pawn is the next step to improving his or her game. For this I recomend the following book for grades 5 and up:

- *How To Think Ahead in Chess* by I. A. Horowitz & Fred Reinfeld. Published by Simon and Schuster, Inc. This book teaches players to make good developing moves for games started with the King-pawn or the Queen-pawn. Part One discussed playing with the white pieces, and Part Two discusses playing with the black pieces.

Players should now be ready to tackle combination play. The combination is a series of moves which results in a material or positional advantage. For this I recommend the following book:

- *The Basis of Combination in Chess* by J. Du Mont. Published by Dover Publications, Inc. This book covers the principles of combination play. Du Mont discusses one piece at a time, then shows how to team up the chess pieces for good combination play.

In order to improve, players need to have a more complete understanding of the basics of chess. For this I recommend the following book:

- *The ABCs of Chess* by Bruce Pandolfini. Published by Simon & Schuster, Inc. Bruce Pandolfini is a professional chess teacher. This is an excellent instructional book which will give players a more complete understanding of the basics of chess.

Intermediate Players:

Players should not limit themselves to King-pawn or Queen-pawn openings. In order to improve their game they need to study a variety of opening moves. I recommend the following books for Jr. High and up:

- There are several good books on different types of openings. However, I would like to mention the following book, because it includes the history of the various chess openings, which I found very interesting:

- **Dynamic Chess** by R. N. Coles. Published by Dover Publications, Inc. This book covers the development of chess strategy from its beginnings, with the classic style, to the Hypermodern ideas, to Russian chess. Different types of openings through the history of chess are explained. This book also includes a collection of games of several great chess players. These games illustrate each player's strategy and style of play, and are very instructive.

Players who want a deeper understanding of chess which will teach them to create a winning plan, will benefit from the following books:

- **The Complete Chessplayer** by Fred Reinfeld. Published by Prentice Hall, Inc. This book will give the chessplayer a solid, complete understanding of the game, which will enable the player to develop crucial planning skills.

- **How to Reassess Your Chess** by Jeremy Silman. Published by Thinkers Press in Davenport, Iowa. This book teaches excellent "thinking techniques" which teaches the chessplayer how to create plans in a chess game. The book also contains valuable information on how to effectively use your knights and bishops throughout the game.

Advanced Players:

Advanced players will benefit from learning Nimzovich's theories of positional chess. I recommend his book for High School and up:

- **My System** by Aron Nimzovich. Published by David McKay Company, Inc. Aron Nimzovich's ideas contributed significantly to modern chess strategy. His book is considered to be one of the best chess books ever written.

BIBLIOGRAPHY

School Mates. Vol.3 No.4 Winter 1989, U.S. Chess Federation. This magazine was my source of information for the chess clock.

Pandolfini, Bruce. *The ABCs of Chess.* Simon & Schuster, Inc., 1986. This book was my source of information for open and closed games, weak pawns, pawn structure, and speed chess.

Reinfeld, Fred. *The Complete Chessplayer.* Prentice Hall Press, 1987. This book was my source of information for rules, checkmating the enemy king, attacking techniques, defensive strategy, understanding pawn structure and weak squares, and understanding material and positional advantages.

Silman, Jeremy. *How to Reassess Your Chess.* Thinkers' Press, 1991. This book was my source of information for understanding knights and bishops.

Nimzovich, Aron. *My System.* David McKay Company, 1989. This book was my source of information for blockades, over-protection, and pawn chains.

U.S. CHESS FEDERATION

The annual fees are as of October 1994—prices subject to change without notification.

The U.S. Chess Federation offers the following types of memberships:

1) Scholastic (Age 19 or under). You get six issues of *School Mates* (for beginners) a year. $7.00.

2) Youth (Age 19 or under). You get the monthly magazine *Chess Life* (for advanced players) for a year. $15.00.

3) Youth (Age 19 or under). You can subscribe to *School Mates* and *Chess Life* for a year. $22.50.

4) Adult Membership. You get *Chess Life* for a year. $30.00.

Other membership benefits include:

- Membership card which entitles you to play in tournaments and earn a national rating.

- U.S. Chess Catalog for books and chess equipment.

- A list of state organizations and affiliated chess clubs in your area (on request).

- Postal chess.

* An annual subscription to *School Mates* for non-members is $7.50.

To join the U.S. Chess Federation, send type of membership selected, annual fee, your full name, complete address, and birth date to:

U.S. Chess Federation
186 Route 9W
New Windsor, NY 12553

or to join by credit card, phone:
1-800-388-KING

Part 3
Answers to Problems

Answer—En Passant Rule

Problem 1:

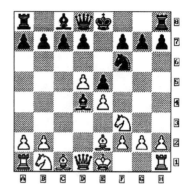

Black to move.

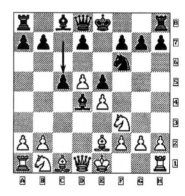

Black moves c pawn two spaces. Can white capture black's c pawn?

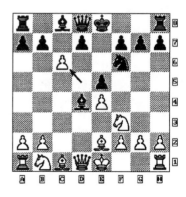

Answer: Yes. White's d pawn can capture black's c pawn en passant "on his next move only."

REMEMBER: The pawn on its fifth rank has the en passant option on his next move only. If this option is not used on his next move, the option is lost.

Answers—Castling

Problem 2:

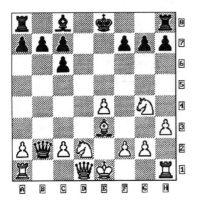

White to move. Can white castle?

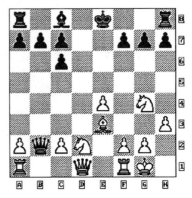

Answer: Yes.

Problem 3:

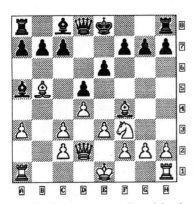

Black to move. Can black castle?

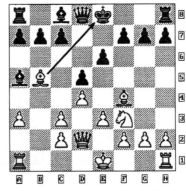

Answer: No. Black is in check. Black can move his bishop to d7 to block the check and may castle later; or black can move his king out of check, in which case he can no longer castle during this game.

Problem 4: Black to move. Can black castle?

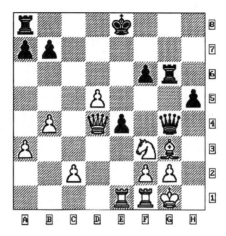

Answer: Yes. Square b8 is under attack, but the king does not pass through this square.

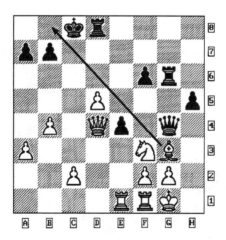

REMEMBER: There are certain restrictions for castling:

1) The pieces between the king and rook have been moved, and these squares are vacant.

2) Neither the king nor the rook have been previously moved.

3) The king must not be in check or pass through a square that is under attack.

Answers—Perpetual Check

Problem 5: Black to move. Can black keep white in perpetual check?

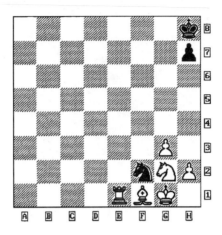

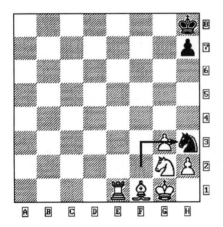
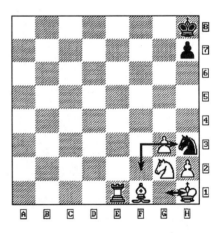

Answer: Yes. Black does not have much chance of winning, so he is wise to put white's king in perpetual check. This will end the game in a draw.

Problem 6: Black to move. Can black keep white in perpetual check?

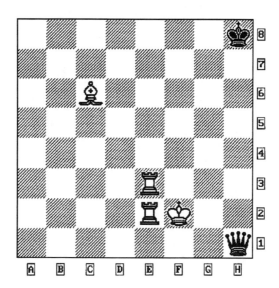

Answer: No. White's king can move to f3 or to e1 to escape black's queen.

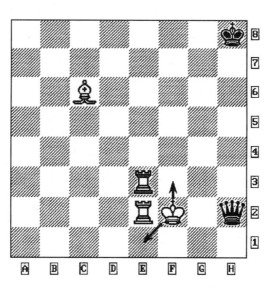

Answers—Stalemate

Problem 7:

Black to move. Is this stalemate?

Answer: Yes.

Problem 8: White to move. Is this stalemate?

Answer: No. White's king can move to c1.

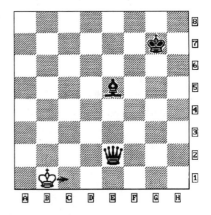

Problem 9: White to move. Is this stalemate?

Answer: Yes.

Problem 10: White to move. Is this stalemate?

Answer: No. White's king can move to a2.

Problem 11: Black to move. Is this stalemate?

Answer: Yes.

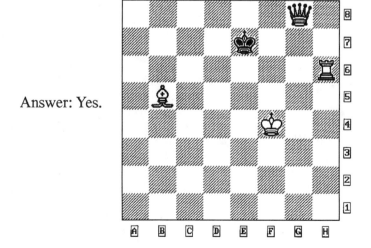

Answers—Pins

Problem 12:

White to move. Black has forked white's rook and knight. Look for a pin that will prevent black from winning one of white's pieces.

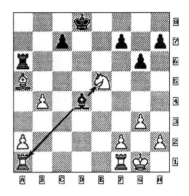

Answer: Rook to d1.

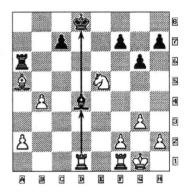

Problem 13:

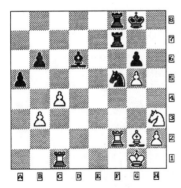

Black to move. Look for the pin.

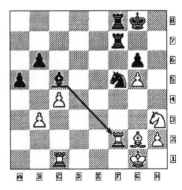

Answer: Bishop to c5 pins the rook against the king.

Problem 14: White to move. Look for the move that takes advantage of a pin which already exists.

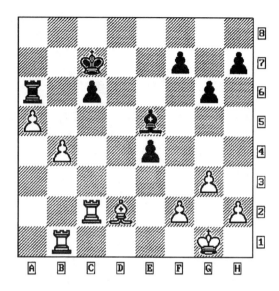

Answer: Pawn to b5. Black's c pawn is pinned against his king and cannot attack white's pawn on b5.

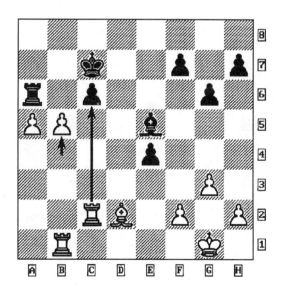

Answers—Forks

Problem 15: Black to move. Look for the move that will fork two of white's pieces.

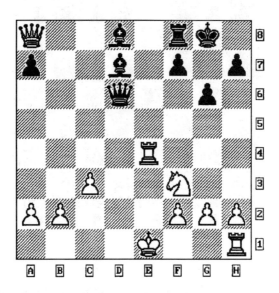

Answer: Bishop to c6 attacks white's queen and rook.

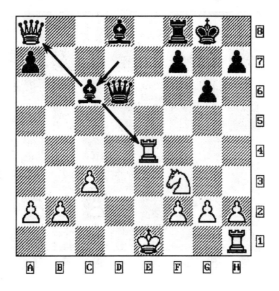

Problem 16:
White to move. Look for a forking move using one of the knights.

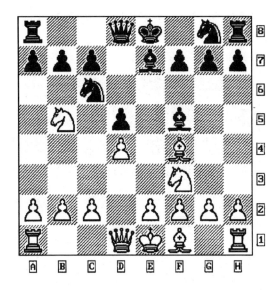

Answer: N captures c7. This puts the king in check and also attacks the rook. The knight at c7 is protected by white's bishop at f4. If black's queen takes white's knight, white's bishop will take black's queen.

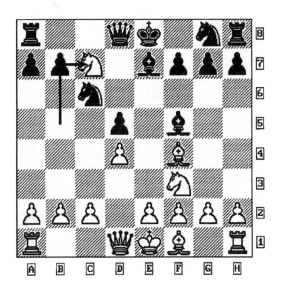

Problem 17: Black to move. Look for a powerful forking move.

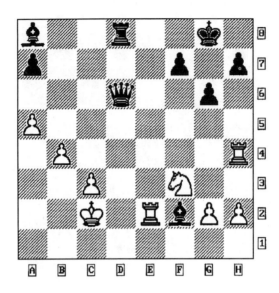

Answer: Black's queen to d1 puts white's king in check and attacks white's rook. White's king cannot take black's queen as it is protected by black's rook on d8.

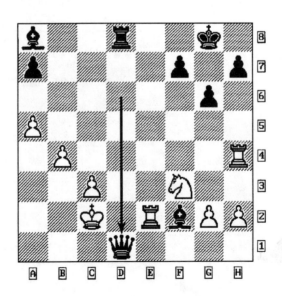